Sometimes things start as a good
idea but can be a bad idea.
And sometimes ideas need
to be thought about.

Meet
James, Ari, and Aiden

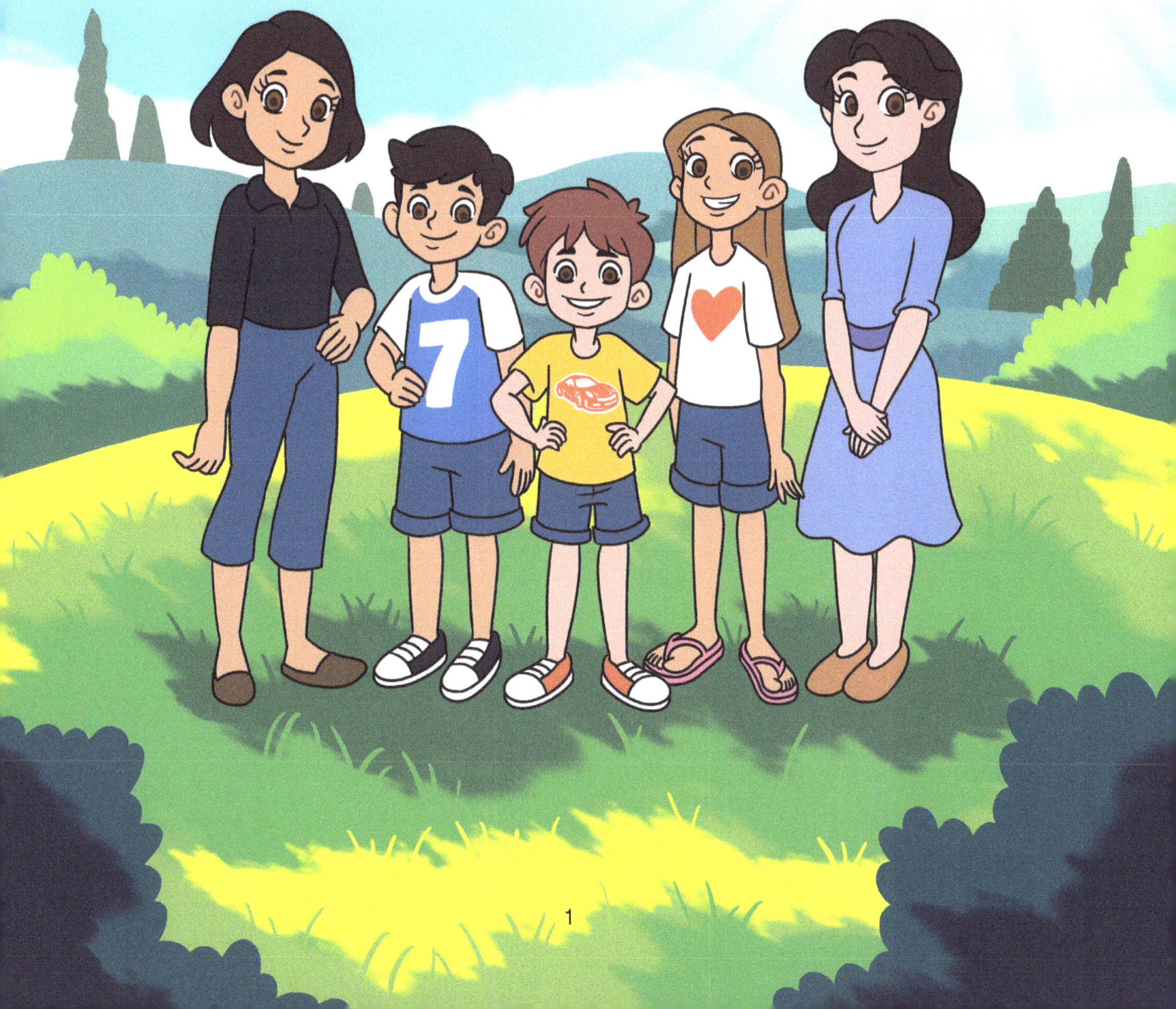

Good Idea,
Bad Idea,
Why?
M. D. Morin

ISBN 979-8-88685-731-3 (paperback)
ISBN 979-8-88685-732-0 (digital)

Copyright © 2023 by M. D. Morin

All rights reserved. No part of this publication may be reproduced, distributed, or transmitted in any form or by any means, including photocopying, recording, or other electronic or mechanical methods without the prior written permission of the publisher. For permission requests, solicit the publisher via the address below.

Christian Faith Publishing
832 Park Avenue
Meadville, PA 16335
www.christianfaithpublishing.com

Printed in the United States of America

Not too long ago, a little boy named Aiden went to visit his cousins James and Ari. When Aiden and his mother arrived, everyone was already outside on the porch enjoying the beautiful, fresh, warm Saturday afternoon.

Immediately the kids were very excited to see one another.

"Mom... Mom! Can we stay and play outside?" Aiden shouted in excitement.

"Yes, as long as you three are careful, and be sure to drink plenty of water," his mother replied.

The three were quick to flee, as their mothers remained on the porch.

"What game shall we play?" asked Ari.

"How about hide-and-seek?" said James.

"That sounds great!" replied Aiden.

"I'll count," James said excitedly.

7

As James counted to one hundred, Ari and Aiden ran off to hide.

Aiden whispered, "There, under Mom's parked car."

"No, that's not a good idea. What if your mom has to go to the store? We could be run over," responded Ari.

Aiden agreed.

"Well, what about behind the car? We could hide there? asked Aiden.

"No, that's a bad idea also. We are short and can't be seen by the mirrors of the car," said Ari.
"Can we hide inside the car?" questioned Aiden with a puzzled look.

"Sorry, Aiden, but that's a bad idea again. On a warm day, the inside of a car can be as hot as an oven when the windows and doors are closed," explained Ari.

"Tag! You're it!" yelled James. Ari and Aiden jumped as James tagged Ari.

"Now you have to count to a hundred. Let's go and hide, Aiden," said James.
And they both ran off.

James saw a ladder leaning on the side of the house.
    "Let's climb the ladder and get on the roof," said James with a soft voice.

    "No, we can't do that. It's a bad idea. We could fall off and get hurt," Aiden said, shaking his head.

"What about the crawl space over here?"
"Not at all. There could be snakes, spiders, or loose wires in there."

13

7

"Let's go hide in the tool shed out back! It's unlocked, and no one will find us in there." James pointed at the shed.

"No, that's not a good idea. There are too many dangerous tools in there."

"Fine, where can we hide?"
James cried in frustration.

"I think I may have
an idea," Aiden said with
a smirk.

"Let's hide behind the fence and watch her finish counting and follow her," Aiden told James.
"That sounds like a good idea," James said as they both chuckled.

As soon as Ari finished counting, she sprinted to the back of the shed. That sounds like a good place to hide.

She runs to check under the picnic table. That sounds like a good idea to hide.

As James and Aiden hid, Ari spotted them through the glass door.

Ari sooner spun around the tree.
"Tag! You both are it!" Ari said with a smile.

As soon as Ari tagged both Aiden and James, James's mother exits the glass door with cold drinks for everyone.

7

As soon as everyone finished their drinks, they forgot about hide-and-seek and went inside to build forts instead.

Now that's a great idea.

The end.

About the Author

M. D. Morin is a parent and an advocate for safety. He is a strong believer in educating children in every aspect of life. He is a huge supporter in finding resolutions in helping correct, protect, and raising awareness to children's decisions. He is a concerned father who wants to mold and guide his children to be safety conscious in their choices, which will ultimately help them recognize risks and dangers in their journey in life.

www.ingramcontent.com/pod-product-compliance
Lightning Source LLC
Chambersburg PA
CBHW040158110726
48005CB00018B/2806